contents

GW00367835

NZ, Canada, US and UK readers
Please note that Australian cup and spoon
measurements are metric. A quick conversion
guide appears on page 63.

making dinner fast

This book makes a number of assumptions – first, that you have a few essential ingredients in your pantry: oil, salt, sugar, milk, flour, soy sauce, that sort of thing. It's also a fairly safe bet that a lack of time is your greatest problem; and we're assuming you want to cook fresh, nutritious food for yourself and your family.

Each of the recipes in this book is made using common pantry staples, found in most kitchens, plus four fast ingredients that you can buy in your lunch hour. (In some recipes, you'll need to purchase even fewer than four ingredients.) It's the fastest, easiest way to cook without reverting to packet food or takeaway – perfect for weeknight dinners.

The recipes are laid out so that the ingredients are listed under two headings – *pantry staples* and *what to buy* – so you can see at a glance what you'll need to buy to make tonight's dinner a reality!

elow are the *pantry staples* we assume you have in your kitchen:

Brown sugar	**Oil**	**Pepper**	**Stock**
Butter	olive	**Plain flour**	beef
Garlic	extra virgin olive	**Potatoes**	chicken
Lemons	vegetable	**Salt**	**Wine**
Milk	**Onions**	**Soy sauce**	

chicken, lemon and artichoke skewers

pantry staples
3 medium lemons (420g)
¼ cup (60ml) olive oil

what to buy
600g chicken breast fillets, chopped
2 x 400g cans artichoke hearts, drained, halved
24 button mushrooms

Squeeze juice from 1 lemon (you will need 2 tablespoons juice). Combine juice and oil in a jar and shake well.
Cut remaining lemons into 24 wedges. Thread chicken pieces, artichoke, mushrooms and lemon onto 12 skewers.
Cook skewers on heated lightly oiled grill plate (or grill or barbecue) until browned all over and cooked through. Brush with oil mixture during cooking.

serves 4
per serving 17.8g fat (2.8g saturated); 1417kJ (339 cal); 3.8g carb
tip This recipe can be prepared a day ahead.
on the table in 35 minutes

chicken soup with choy sum

pantry staples
1.5 litres (6 cups) chicken stock
2 tablespoons soy sauce

what to buy
4 single chicken breast fillets (680g), sliced thickly
100g dried rice stick noodles
300g baby choy sum, chopped coarsely

Bring stock to a boil in large saucepan, add chicken; simmer, uncovered, about 5 minutes or until chicken is just cooked through.
Add soy sauce and noodles; simmer, uncovered, about 5 minutes or until noodles are just tender. Add choy sum; simmer, uncovered, until choy sum is just tender.

serves 4
per serving 5.9g fat (1.8g saturated); 1321kJ (316 cal); 19.7g carb
tip This recipe is best made just before serving.
on the table in 25 minutes

creamy pesto chicken with gnocchi

Gnocchi, small Italian "dumplings" usually made from mashed potato or semolina, can be boiled, baked or fried. You need to purchase a large barbecued chicken, weighing approximately 900g, for this recipe.

pantry staples
1 tablespoon olive oil
2 cloves garlic, crushed
½ cup (125ml) dry white wine

what to buy
500g fresh gnocchi
¼ cup (60g) basil pesto
300ml cream
3 cups (400g) coarsely chopped cooked chicken

Cook gnocchi in large saucepan of boiling water, uncovered, about 5 minutes or until gnocchi rise to the surface and are just tender; drain.
Meanwhile, heat oil in large saucepan; cook garlic, stirring, until fragrant. Add wine, pesto and cream; bring to a boil. Reduce heat; simmer, uncovered, 3 minutes.
Add chicken and gnocchi; stir until heated through.
Serve topped with fresh basil leaves, if desired.

serves 4
per serving 46.9g fat (22.8g saturated); 3043kJ (728 cal); 39.1g carb
tip This recipe is best made close to serving time.
on the table in 15 minutes

chicken tikka drumettes

what to buy
12 chicken drumettes (960g)
⅓ cup (100g) tikka masala paste
½ cup (140g) yogurt
¼ cup coarsely chopped fresh coriander

Preheat oven to moderately hot.
Place chicken in large bowl with combined
paste and 2 tablespoons of the yogurt; toss
to coat chicken in paste mixture. Place chicken,
in single layer, on wire rack in large baking dish.
Roast, uncovered, in moderately hot oven about
20 minutes or until chicken is browned and
cooked through.
Meanwhile, combine coriander and remaining
yogurt in small bowl.
Serve chicken drizzled with yogurt mixture,
and accompanied by steamed rice, lime pickle
and pappadums, if desired.

serves 4
per serving 15.5g fat (3.7g saturated);
1166kJ (279 cal); 3.6g carb
tip The chicken can be prepared a day ahead.
on the table in 35 minutes

roast chicken with pea mash and gravy

Who'd ever believe you could have a roast chicken on the table in 30 minutes!
If you have a microwave oven, it's a speedy and simple process.

pantry staples

1 cup (250ml) chicken stock
¾ cup (180ml) dry white wine
3 cloves garlic, crushed
2 large potatoes (600g),
　chopped coarsely
60g butter
2 tablespoons plain flour
1 tablespoon soy sauce

what to buy

1.6kg chicken
2⅓ cups (280g) frozen peas

Preheat conventional oven to very hot.
Using sharp knife or poultry shears, halve chicken lengthways then cut both halves crossways through the centre.
Place chicken, skin-side down, in large microwave-safe dish; pour combined stock, wine and garlic over chicken. Microwave, covered, on HIGH (100%) for 10 minutes.
Carefully transfer chicken from microwave-safe dish to large baking dish in a single layer, skin-side up; pour chicken juices into large jug. Roast chicken, uncovered, in very hot oven about 15 minutes or until browned all over and cooked through.
Meanwhile, boil, steam or microwave potato and peas, separately, until just tender; drain. Mash together in large bowl with half of the butter; cover to keep warm.
Melt remaining butter in medium saucepan; add flour. Cook, stirring, until mixture thickens and bubbles. Gradually stir in reserved chicken juices; stir until mixture boils and thickens. Stir soy sauce into gravy. Serve pea mash with chicken; top with gravy.

serves 4
per serving 41.3g fat (17.1g saturated); 2842kJ (680 cal); 26g carb
tip This recipe is best made close to serving.
on the table in 30 minutes

lemon chicken with garlic pumpkin

pantry staples
2 tablespoons olive oil
4 cloves garlic, sliced thinly
½ cup (125ml) chicken stock
40g butter
1 tablespoon lemon juice

what to buy
800g piece butternut pumpkin, peeled
12 fresh sage leaves
4 single chicken breast fillets (680g)
3 anchovy fillets, drained, chopped finely

Chop pumpkin into 1.5cm cubes. Heat half of
the oil in large saucepan, add pumpkin and garlic;
cook, stirring, until pumpkin begins to brown.
Add 2 tablespoons of the stock; cover and steam
5 minutes or until pumpkin is just tender. Stir in sage.
Meanwhile, cut chicken fillets in half horizontally
to give 8 thin pieces. Melt half of the butter and
remaining oil in large frying pan; add the chicken and
cook until browned on both sides and just cooked
through. Remove chicken from pan and keep warm.
Add remaining butter to same pan with anchovies;
cook, stirring, until butter melts. Add lemon juice
and remaining stock; simmer, uncovered, for
1 minute or until reduced slightly.
Serve pumpkin topped with chicken and sauce.
Serve with rocket or a green salad, if desired.

serves 4
per serving 22.3g fat (8.3g saturated);
1747kJ (418 cal); 11.3g carb
tip This recipe is best made just before serving.
on the table in 25 minutes

15

mussel broth with black bean

pantry staples
1 cup (250ml) water

what to buy
1kg black mussels
⅓ cup (80ml) black bean sauce
2 large fresh red chillies, seeded, sliced thinly
4 green onions, sliced thinly

Scrub mussels; remove beards. Place the water, black bean sauce and chilli in large saucepan; bring to a boil.

Add mussels; cook, covered, about 3 minutes or until mussels open (discard any that remain closed).

Sprinkle with green onion and serve with steamed jasmine rice, if desired.

serves 4
per serving 1.5g fat (0.4g saturated); 297kJ (71 cal); 7.2g carb
tip This recipe is best made close to serving.
on the table in 35 minutes

salt and pepper squid

pantry staples
½ cup (70g) plain flour
2 teaspoons coarse cooking salt
vegetable oil, for deep-frying

what to buy
600g squid hoods
1 tablespoon lemon pepper

Halve squid hoods lengthways, score the
inside in crosshatch pattern then cut each half
lengthways into five pieces. Toss squid in medium
bowl with combined flour, salt and lemon pepper
until coated; shake off excess.
Heat oil in wok or large saucepan; deep-fry
squid, in batches, until tender and browned lightly.
Drain on absorbent paper.
Serve squid with mesclun and mayonnaise,
if desired.

serves 4
per serving 11.6g fat (1.9g saturated);
1112kJ (266 cal); 13.1g carb
tip This recipe is best made just before serving.
on the table in 30 minutes

prawn skewers with lime and green onions

pantry staples
2 tablespoons olive oil
2 cloves garlic, crushed

what to buy
36 medium uncooked prawns (1.5kg)
2 tablespoons lime juice
3 green onions

Peel and devein prawns leaving tails intact.
Combine prawns, lime juice, oil and garlic in large bowl.
Cut green onions into 4cm lengths. Thread 3 prawns onto each of 12 skewers, threading a piece of green onion after each prawn.
Cook skewers in heated oiled grill pan (or grill or barbecue) until browned on both sides and just cooked through.

serves 4
per serving 10.4g fat (1.5g saturated); 1078kJ (258 cal); 1.7g carb
tip The prawns can be marinated in lime mixture for up to 1 hour. If you are using metal skewers, oil them first to prevent the prawns sticking. And don't forget, they will be very hot after cooking. If using bamboo skewers, it is best to soak them in water for at least 1 hour before using.
on the table in 35 minutes

citrus-ginger steamed bream

pantry staples
1 medium lemon (140g)
2 cloves garlic, crushed

what to buy
2 medium oranges (480g)
2cm piece fresh ginger (10g), grated
4 x 250g whole bream, cleaned
⅓ cup loosely packed fresh basil leaves, torn

Using vegetable peeler, peel rind carefully from lemon and one orange; cut rind into thin strips. Squeeze juice of both oranges and lemon into large bowl. Stir in rind, garlic and ginger. Score fish both sides; add to bowl, coat in marinade.
Fold 80cm-long piece of foil in half widthways; place 1 fish on foil, spoon a quarter of the marinade onto fish. Fold foil over fish to tightly enclose. Repeat process with foil, remaining fish and marinade.
Place fish parcels in large steamer fitted over large saucepan of boiling water; steam, covered, about 15 minutes or until cooked through. Sprinkle fish with basil; serve with steamed rice, if desired.

serves 4
per serving 6.6g fat (2.3g saturated);
815kJ (195 cal); 7.5g carb
tip We used whole bream in this recipe, but any fairly small white-fleshed fish can be used. Fish can be marinated for up to 1 hour.
on the table in 35 minutes

pepper-crusted swordfish

pantry staples
1 teaspoon ground white pepper
2 teaspoons cracked black pepper

what to buy
⅓ cup (35g) packaged breadcrumbs
4 x 200g swordfish fillets

Combine peppers and breadcrumbs in small bowl. Press pepper mixture onto one side of each fish fillet.
Cook fish, crumbed-side down, in heated lightly oiled large non-stick frying pan until browned lightly and crisp; turn, cook until browned lightly and cooked through.
Serve fish with steamed potato and beans, if desired.

serves 4
per serving 4.8g fat (1.5g saturated); 995kJ (238 cal); 6.1g carb
tip This recipe is best made just before serving.
on the table in 30 minutes

fish fillets pan-fried with pancetta and caper herb butter

pantry staples
80g butter, softened
2 cloves garlic, quartered
1 tablespoon olive oil

what to buy
⅓ cup coarsely chopped fresh flat-leaf parsley
1 tablespoon capers, rinsed, drained
8 slices pancetta (120g)
4 white fish fillets (600g)

Blend or process butter, parsley, capers and garlic until mixture forms a smooth paste.
Spread a quarter of the butter mixture and two slices of the pancetta on each fish fillet.
Heat oil in large heavy-based frying pan; cook fish, pancetta-side down, until pancetta is crisp. Turn fish carefully; cook, uncovered, until cooked through.
Serve fish drizzled with pan juices and steamed asparagus, if desired.

serves 4
per serving 26g fat (13.2g saturated); 1576kJ (377 cal); 0.7g carb
tip We used snapper fillets for this recipe, but any firm white fish fillet can be used.
on the table in 25 minutes

bistro pepper steaks with fries

pantry staples
1 teaspoon salt
1 tablespoon olive oil
1½ cups (375ml) beef stock

what to buy
1kg frozen potato fries or chips
2 tablespoons peppercorn medley
4 beef scotch fillet steaks (600g)
⅓ cup (80ml) thickened cream

Prepare fries or chips according to packet instructions.
Meanwhile, place pepper and salt in shallow dish; press onto both sides of steaks.
Heat oil in large frying pan; cook steaks until browned on both sides and cooked as desired. Remove from pan; cover to keep warm.
Add stock to pan; simmer, uncovered, until reduced by half. Stir in cream.
Serve steaks with sauce and chips.

serves 4
per serving 43.7g fat (16.5g saturated); 4301kJ (1029 cal); 112.4g carb
tip This recipe is best made close to serving.
on the table in 25 minutes

lemon and rosemary veal cutlets

pantry staples
2 tablespoons finely grated lemon rind
2 tablespoons olive oil
2 tablespoons lemon juice
1 clove garlic, crushed

what to buy
1 tablespoon finely chopped fresh rosemary
4 x 200g veal cutlets, trimmed
1kg kipfler potatoes
4 green onions, sliced thinly

Combine rosemary, rind and oil in small jug, place half of the mixture in medium bowl with veal; toss to coat veal in mixture.
Boil, steam or microwave unpeeled potatoes until just tender; drain. Quarter potatoes lengthways.
Stir juice and garlic into reserved remaining marinade.
Cook veal in heated lightly oiled large non-stick frying pan until browned both sides and cooked as desired.
Meanwhile, place potato and onion in large bowl; toss salad gently to combine. Serve veal on salad; drizzle with reserved marinade mixture.

serves 4
per serving 12.4g fat (2.2g saturated); 1651kJ (395 cal); 34g carb
tip The veal can be marinated overnight.
on the table in 35 minutes

31

chilli T-bone steak with hash browns

pantry staples
3 medium potatoes (600g)
40g butter
1 small brown onion (80g), chopped finely

what to buy
4 beef T-bone steaks (1.2kg)
⅓ cup (80ml) worcestershire sauce
⅓ cup (80ml) hot chilli sauce

Combine steaks and sauces in large bowl;
toss to coat steaks all over in marinade.
Meanwhile, grate peeled potatoes coarsely. Using
hands, squeeze excess liquid from potato; spread
onto sheets of absorbent paper, squeeze again to
remove as much liquid as possible from potato.
Heat half of the butter in large non-stick frying pan;
cook onion, stirring, until soft. Add potato; stir over
heat constantly until potato begins to stick to pan.
Remove from heat; cool 5 minutes. Transfer
potato mixture to large bowl.
Using wet hands, shape potato mixture into
eight patties. Heat remaining butter in same pan;
cook hash browns, in batches, until browned and
crisp on both sides. Drain on absorbent paper.
Drain steaks; discard marinade. Cook steaks, in
batches, on heated oiled grill plate (or grill or barbecue)
until browned both sides and cooked as desired.
Serve steaks with hash browns and salad, if desired.

serves 4
per serving 20.3g fat (10.3g saturated);
1931kJ (462 cal); 25.4g carb
on the table in 35 minutes

veal parmesan

pantry staples
1 tablespoon olive oil

what to buy
4 large veal steaks (500g)
1 cup (250ml) bottled tomato pasta sauce
1 cup (100g) grated mozzarella cheese
½ cup (40g) grated parmesan cheese

Heat oil in large frying pan; cook veal until browned lightly and cooked as desired. Transfer veal to shallow ovenproof dish.
Add sauce to same reheated frying pan; cook until heated through. Spoon sauce over veal, top with cheeses; grill until cheese melts and is browned.

serves 4
per serving 16.8g fat (7.2g saturated); 1392kJ (333 cal); 7.4g carb
tip This recipe is best made just before serving.
on the table in 35 minutes

veal cutlets with anchovy garlic butter

pantry staples
1 lemon
2 cloves garlic, crushed
¼ cup (60ml) extra virgin olive oil
1 clove garlic, crushed, extra
125g butter, softened

what to buy
8 small veal cutlets (1.3kg)
1 tablespoon fresh sage leaves
4 anchovy fillets, drained
1 teaspoon finely chopped fresh sage, extra

Peel rind thinly from lemon using a vegetable peeler. Cut rind into long, thin strips.
Combine cutlets, garlic, sage leaves, rind and oil in large bowl; toss to coat cutlets, stand 10 minutes.
Meanwhile, pound or chop anchovy and extra garlic together to form a paste. Beat butter in a bowl with a wooden spoon until smooth; beat in anchovy paste and extra sage until combined.
Cook cutlets on heated oiled grill plate (or grill or barbecue) until browned on both sides and cooked as desired.
Serve cutlets with anchovy butter and a mixed salad, if desired.

serves 4
per serving 45.6g fat (20.7g saturated); 2730kJ (653 cal); 0.9g carb
tip The veal can be marinated, and the anchovy butter made, a day ahead.
on the table in 35 minutes

honey and soy roast pork

pantry staples
1 tablespoon soy sauce

what to buy
2 large pork fillets (750g)
750g kumara, sliced thickly
1 tablespoon wholegrain mustard
2 tablespoons honey

Preheat oven to very hot.
Cut each pork fillet in half. Place pork and
kumara in an oiled baking dish. Pour over
combined mustard, honey and soy sauce,
toss to coat pork and kumara in honey mixture.
Bake pork and kumara, uncovered, in very hot
oven about 25 minutes or until cooked through.
Slice pork and serve with kumara and a crisp
rocket salad, if desired.

serves 4
per serving 4.6g fat (1.5g saturated);
1526kJ (365 cal); 36g carb
tip For a more intense flavour, marinate the pork
in half of the mustard mixture overnight.
on the table in 30 minutes

pork with white bean puree

pantry staples
2 tablespoons olive oil
2 cloves garlic, quartered
1 tablespoon lemon juice

what to buy
4 x 250g pork cutlets
250g cherry tomatoes
2 x 300g can butter beans, rinsed, drained

Brush pork and tomatoes with half of the oil; cook pork and tomatoes on heated oiled grill plate (or grill or barbecue) until pork is browned on both sides and cooked through, and tomatoes are soft.

Meanwhile, place beans in medium saucepan, cover with water; bring to a boil, then simmer, uncovered, until beans are heated through. Drain well.

Blend or process beans with remaining oil, garlic and juice until smooth.

Serve pork with tomatoes, white bean puree and lemon wedges, if desired.

serves 4
per serving 32.8g fat (9.4g saturated); 2027kJ (485 cal); 3.7g carb
tip The white bean puree can be made a day ahead.
on the table in 30 minutes

teriyaki pork stir-fry

pantry staples
1 clove garlic, crushed

what to buy
750g pork fillets, sliced thinly
6 green onions, chopped finely
3 baby bok choy (450g), chopped coarsely
⅓ cup (80ml) teriyaki marinade

Cook pork, in batches, in heated oiled wok or large frying pan, until browned all over and cooked through; remove from wok.
Cook onion and garlic in same wok, stirring, until fragrant. Return pork to wok with bok choy; cook, stirring, until bok choy is wilted.
Add teriyaki marinade; cook until heated through.

serves 4
per serving 4.6g fat (1.5g saturated); 953kJ (228 cal); 2.3g carb
tip This recipe is best made just before serving.
on the table in 20 minutes

grilled lamb and risoni with mustard sauce

Risoni is a small rice-shaped pasta that can be served similarly to orzo or rice in salads and soups.

pantry staples
1 tablespoon olive oil
2 cloves garlic, crushed

what to buy
450g lamb fillets
500g risoni
300ml cream
¼ cup (70g) wholegrain mustard

Cook lamb, in batches, on heated oiled grill plate (or grill or barbecue) until browned and cooked as desired. Cover; stand 5 minutes, slice thickly.
Meanwhile, cook pasta in large saucepan of boiling water, uncovered, until just tender.
Heat oil in small saucepan; cook garlic, stirring, until fragrant. Add cream and mustard; bring to a boil. Reduce heat; simmer, uncovered, 2 minutes.
Place drained pasta, lamb and sauce in large bowl; toss gently to combine.

serves 4
per serving 44g fat (23.6g saturated); 3862kJ (924 cal); 91.4g carb
tip This recipe is best made just before serving.
on the table in 35 minutes

tandoori lamb cutlets

pantry staples
1 medium lemon (140g)
2 teaspoons brown sugar

what to buy
12 lamb cutlets (780g)
¼ cup (75g) tandoori paste
¼ cup (70g) yogurt

Grate rind finely from lemon and squeeze juice; you will need 1 teaspoon rind and 1 tablespoon juice.
Place lamb cutlets in large bowl with rind, juice, paste, yogurt and sugar. Cover; stand 10 minutes.
Cook lamb on heated oiled grill plate (or grill or barbecue) until browned both sides and cooked as desired.
Serve with steamed basmati rice and lemon wedges, if desired.

serves 4
per serving 15.1g fat (4.9g saturated); 1020kJ (244 cal); 4.3g carb
tip The cutlets can be marinated overnight.
on the table in 30 minutes

47

lamb with white wine and mascarpone sauce

pantry staples
2 tablespoons olive oil
1 clove garlic, crushed
¾ cup (180ml) dry white wine

what to buy
100g prosciutto
8 lamb steaks (640g)
½ cup (125g) mascarpone
¼ cup (60ml) cream

Heat oil in medium frying pan; cook prosciutto, stirring, until crisp. Drain on absorbent paper.
Cook lamb in same pan until browned both sides and cooked as desired. Remove from pan.
Cook garlic in same pan, stirring, until fragrant. Add wine; bring to a boil. Reduce heat; simmer, uncovered, until liquid reduces by half. Add mascarpone and cream; cook, stirring, until sauce boils and thickens slightly.
Divide lamb among serving plates; top with prosciutto, drizzle with sauce.
Serve with steamed asparagus, if desired.

serves 4
per serving 48.1g fat (23.6g saturated); 2579kJ (617 cal); 1.3g carb
tip This recipe is best made just before serving.
on the table in 25 minutes

balsamic and rosemary lamb

pantry staples
2 tablespoons olive oil

what to buy
¼ cup (60ml) balsamic vinegar
1 tablespoon fresh rosemary leaves
12 lamb cutlets (780g)

Combine oil, vinegar and rosemary in medium bowl, add lamb; toss lamb to coat in marinade, stand 10 minutes.
Drain lamb; discard marinade. Cook lamb on heated oiled grill plate, uncovered, until cooked as desired.

serves 4
per serving 17.7g fat (5.2g saturated); 1007kJ (241 cal); 0g carb
tip The lamb can be marinated overnight.
on the table in 30 minutes

linguine al pesto

pantry staples
2 cloves garlic, peeled, quartered
½ cup (125ml) olive oil

what to buy
500g linguine
2 cups firmly packed fresh basil leaves
½ cup (40g) coarsely grated parmesan cheese
⅓ cup (50g) toasted pine nuts

Cook pasta in large saucepan of boiling water, uncovered, until just tender.
Meanwhile, blend or process basil, garlic, cheese and nuts with a little of the olive oil. When basil mixture is just pureed, gradually pour in remaining oil with motor operating; blend until mixture forms a paste.
Drain pasta. Combine pasta in large bowl with pesto; toss gently.

serves 4
per serving 41.9g fat (6.9g saturated); 3398kJ (813 cal); 88.8g carb
tip The pesto freezes well so it will see you through the winter if you make several quantities of this recipe when basil is in season.
on the table in 30 minutes

cheese and spinach tortellini with gorgonzola sauce

Gorgonzola is a traditional northern Italian creamy blue cheese. The double-cream Bavarian blue or Blue Castello can be substituted, but will lack that particular tempered piquancy of a ripe gorgonzola.

pantry staples
30g butter
2 tablespoons plain flour
1 cup (250ml) milk

what to buy
750g cheese and spinach tortellini
¾ cup (180ml) cream
100g gorgonzola cheese, chopped coarsely
¼ cup loosely packed fresh flat-leaf parsley

Cook pasta in large saucepan of boiling water, uncovered, until just tender.
Meanwhile, melt butter in medium saucepan, add flour; cook, stirring, about 2 minutes or until mixture thickens and bubbles.
Gradually stir in milk and cream; bring to a boil. Reduce heat; simmer, uncovered, until sauce boils and thickens. Remove from heat; stir in cheese.
Combine drained pasta and sauce; sprinkle with parsley to serve.

serves 4
per serving 41.6g fat (26.6g saturated); 3064kJ (733 cal); 63.1g carb
tip You can substitute the tortellini with ravioli or even gnocchi, if you prefer.
on the table in 20 minutes

fettuccine with char-grilled vegetables

what to buy
500g fettuccine
2 x 280g jars antipasto char-grilled vegetables
200g baby spinach leaves
1 cup (80g) parmesan cheese flakes

Cook pasta in large saucepan of boiling water, uncovered, until just tender; drain.
Meanwhile, drain vegetables; reserve ¼ cup (60ml) of oil. Chop vegetables coarsely; in same pan, cook vegetables and reserved oil until hot.
Toss hot pasta with vegetable mixture, spinach and half of the cheese. To serve, top with remaining cheese.

serves 4
per serving 28.7g fat (6.9g saturated); 3035kJ (726 cal); 92.6g carb
tip This recipe is best made just before serving.
on the table in 20 minutes

vegetable pesto tartlets

what to buy
2 sheets ready rolled butter puff pastry, thawed
½ cup (130g) sun-dried tomato pesto
280g jar antipasto char-grilled vegetables
150g fetta cheese, crumbled

Preheat oven to very hot.
Cut pastry sheets in half. Place the four pastry pieces on two oven trays. Fold pastry edges in to make a 1cm border. Spread pesto over centre of pastry.
Drain vegetables; pat dry with absorbent paper. Cut vegetables into strips. Arrange vegetables on pastry pieces; sprinkle with cheese.
Bake, uncovered, in very hot oven 10 minutes. Swap shelf position of trays; bake 10 minutes or until pastry is puffed and browned. To serve, top with small basil leaves, if desired.

serves 4
per serving 44.1g fat (19g saturated); 2437kJ (583 cal); 32.6g carb
tip This recipe is best made just before serving.
on the table in 35 minutes

glossary

artichoke hearts tender centre of the globe artichoke. Artichoke hearts can be harvested fresh from the plant or purchased in brine, canned, or in glass jars.

balsamic vinegar there are many balsamic vinegars on the market ranging in pungency and quality depending on how, and how long, they have been aged. Quality can be determined up to a point by price; use the most expensive sparingly.

basil we used sweet basil, unless otherwise specified.

beef

scotch fillet steak: also known as beef rib-eye steaks.

T-bone steak: sirloin steak with the bone in and fillet eye attached; also known as porterhouse.

black bean sauce a Chinese sauce made from fermented soy beans, spices, water and wheat flour.

bok choy also known as bak choy, pak choi, chinese white cabbage or chinese chard; has a fresh, mild mustard taste. Use stems and leaves, stir-fried or braised. Baby bok choy, also known as pak kat farang, shanghai bok choy, chinese chard or white cabbage, is small and more tender than bok choy.

breadcrumbs, packaged fine-textured, crunchy, purchased white breadcrumbs.

butter use salted or unsalted (sweet) butter; 125g is equal to one stick of butter.

butter beans, canned cans labelled butter beans are, in fact, cannellini beans. "Butter" is also another name for lima beans, sold both dried and canned; a large beige bean having a mealy texture and mild taste.

capers sold either dried and salted or pickled in a vinegar brine; tiny, young baby capers are also available.

cheese

fetta: a crumbly textured goat or sheep milk cheese with a sharp, salty taste.

gorgonzola: creamy Italian blue cheese with mild, sweet taste.

mascarpone: cheese variety that is whitish to creamy yellow in colour, with a soft, creamy texture.

mozzarella: soft spun-curd cheese; it has a low melting point and elastic texture when heated and is used to add texture rather than flavour.

parmesan: also known as parmigiano; a hard, grainy cow-milk cheese. The curd is salted in brine for a month before being aged for up to two years in humid conditions.

chicken

breast fillets: breast halved, skinned and boned.

drumettes: the small fleshy part of a chicken wing between the shoulder and elbow.

chilli available in many different types and sizes. Use rubber gloves when seeding and chopping fresh chillies as they can burn your skin. Removing the seeds and membranes lessens the heat level.

hot chilli sauce: we used a hot Chinese variety made from birdseye chillies, salt and vinegar.

choy sum also known as pakaukeo or flowering cabbage, a member of the bok choy family; easy to identify with its long stems, light green leaves and yellow flowers. Is completely edible, stems and all.

coriander also known as pak chee, cilantro or chinese parsley; bright-green leafy herb with a pungent flavour. Both the stems and roots of coriander can be used.

cream, thickened (minimum fat content 35%) whipping cream containing a thickener.

flour, plain an all-purpose flour, made from wheat.

ginger, fresh also known as green or root ginger; the thick gnarled root of a tropical plant.

gnocchi Italian "dumplings" made of potatoes, and semolina or flour.

kumara Polynesian name for orange-fleshed sweet potato often confused with yam.

lamb

cutlet: small, tender rib chop.

fillet: the smaller piece of meat from a row of loin chops or cutlets.

lemon pepper also known as lemon pepper seasoning. A blend of crushed black pepper, lemon, herbs and spices.

mushrooms, button small, cultivated white mushrooms with a mild flavour.

mussels, black must be tightly closed when bought; this is an indication they are alive. Before cooking, scrub the shells with a strong brush and remove "beards". Discard any that don't open when cooked.

mustard, wholegrain also known as seeded. A French-style coarse-grain mustard made from crushed mustard seeds and dijon-style French mustard.

noodles, dried rice stick also known as sen lek, ho fun or kway teow. Come in different widths – should be soaked in hot water until soft.

oil

olive: made from ripened olives. Extra virgin and virgin are the first and second press, respectively, of the olives and are therefore considered the best, while extra light or light is diluted and refers to taste not fat levels.

vegetable: any of a number of oils sourced from plants rather than animal fats.

onion

green: also known as scallion or (incorrectly) shallot; an immature onion picked before the bulb has formed, having a long, bright-green edible stalk.

pancetta cured pork belly; bacon can be substituted.

parsley, flat-leaf also known as continental parsley and italian parsley.

peppercorn medley most commonly a blend of black, white, pink and green peppercorns. Available from supermarkets and specialty stores.

pine nuts also known as pignoli; not in fact a nut but a small, cream-coloured kernel from pine cones.

pork fillet skinless, boneless eye-fillet cut from the loin.

potato, kipfler small, finger-shaped, nutty flavour; great baked and in salads.

prawns also known as shrimp.

prosciutto salt-cured, air-dried (unsmoked) pressed ham; usually sold in paper-thin slices, ready to eat.

pumpkin also known as squash.

ready rolled puff pastry packaged sheets of frozen pastry, available from supermarkets.

risoni small rice-shaped pasta.

rosemary Mediterranean herb with a strong, aromatic flavour. Sold fresh or dried.

sage pungent herb with narrow, grey-green leaves; slightly bitter with a musty mint aroma. Sold fresh or dried.

soy sauce made from fermented soy beans. Several variations are available in most supermarkets and Asian food stores.

spinach also known as english spinach and, incorrectly, silverbeet.

squid a type of mollusc; also known as calamari. Buy squid hoods to make preparation easier.

stock 1 cup (250ml) stock is the equivalent of 1 cup (250ml) water plus 1 crumbled stock cube (or 1 teaspoon stock powder).

sugar, brown an extremely soft, fine granulated sugar retaining molasses for its characteristic colour and flavour.

sun-dried tomato pesto a thick paste made from sun-dried tomatoes, oil and herbs.

tandoori paste a blend consisting of garlic, tamarind, ginger, coriander, chilli and spices.

teriyaki marinade a bottled sauce usually made from soy sauce, mirin, sugar, ginger and other spices.

tikka masala paste a blend consisting of chilli, coriander, cumin, lentil flour, garlic, ginger, oil, turmeric, fennel, pepper, cloves, cinnamon and cardamom.

tomato

cherry: also known as Tiny Tim or Tom Thumb tomatoes; small and round.

pasta sauce: a prepared tomato-based sauce; comes in varying degrees of thickness and types of spicing.

tortellini circles of fresh plain pasta that are stuffed with a meat or cheese filling, and then folded into little "hat" shapes.

wine never cook with wine you wouldn't drink; we used good-quality dry white and red wine in our recipes.

worcestershire sauce a thin, dark-brown spicy sauce used as a seasoning.

yogurt we used unflavoured full-fat yogurt in our recipes, unless otherwise specified.

index

facts & figures

These conversions are approximate only, but the difference between an exact and the approximate conversion of various liquid and dry measures is minimal and will not affect your cooking results.

Note: NZ, Canada, US and UK all use 15ml tablespoons. Australian tablespoons measure 20ml. All cup and spoon measurements are level.

Measuring equipment

The difference between one country's measuring cups and another's is, at most, within a 2 or 3 teaspoon variance. (For the record, 1 Australian metric measuring cup holds approximately 250ml.) The most accurate way of measuring dry ingredients is to weigh them. For liquids, use a clear glass or plastic jug having metric markings.

How to measure

When using graduated measuring cups, shake dry ingredients loosely into the appropriate cup. Do not tap the cup on a bench or tightly pack the ingredients unless directed to do so. Level the top of measuring cups and measuring spoons with a knife. When measuring liquids, place a clear glass or plastic jug having metric markings on a flat surface to check accuracy at eye level.

Dry measures

metric	imperial
15g	½oz
30g	1oz
60g	2oz
90g	3oz
125g	4oz (¼lb)
155g	5oz
185g	6oz
220g	7oz
250g	8oz (½lb)
280g	9oz
315g	10oz
345g	11oz
375g	12oz (¾lb)
410g	13oz
440g	14oz
470g	15oz
500g	16oz (1lb)
750g	24oz (1½lb)
1kg	32oz (2lb)

We use large eggs with an average weight of 60g.

Liquid measures

metric	imperial
30 ml	1 fluid oz
60 ml	2 fluid oz
100 ml	3 fluid oz
125 ml	4 fluid oz
150 ml	5 fluid oz (¼ pint/1 gill)
190 ml	6 fluid oz
250 ml (1cup)	8 fluid oz
300 ml	10 fluid oz (½ pint)
500 ml	16 fluid oz
600 ml	20 fluid oz (1 pint)
1000 ml (1litre)	1¾ pints

Helpful measures

metric	imperial
3mm	⅛in
6mm	¼in
1cm	½in
2cm	¾in
2.5cm	1in
6cm	2½in
8cm	3in
20cm	8in
23cm	9in
25cm	10in
30cm	12in (1ft)

Oven temperatures

These oven temperatures are only a guide. Always check the manufacturer's manual.

	°C (Celsius)	°F (Fahrenheit)	Gas Mark
Very slow	120	250	½
Slow	140 – 150	275 – 300	1 – 2
Moderately slow	170	325	3
Moderate	180 –190	350 – 375	4 – 5
Moderately hot	200	400	6
Hot	220 – 230	425 – 450	7 – 8
Very hot	240	475	9

at your fingertips

These elegant slipcovers store up to 12 mini books and make the books instantly accessible.

And the metric measuring cups and spoons make following our recipes a piece of cake.

Book Holder
Australia and overseas:
$8.95 (incl. GST).

Metric Measuring Set
Australia: $6.50 (incl. GST).
New Zealand: $A8.00.
Elsewhere: $A9.95.
Prices include postage and handling. This offer is available in all countries.

Mail or fax Photocopy and complete the coupon below and post to ACP Books Reader Offer, ACP Publishing, GPO Box 4967, Sydney NSW 2001, or fax to (02) 9267 4967.

Phone Have your credit card details ready, then phone 136 116 (Mon-Fri, 8.00am-6.00pm; Sat, 8.00am-6.00pm).

Australian residents We accept the credit cards listed on the coupon, money orders and cheques.

Overseas residents We accept the credit cards listed on the coupon, drafts in $A drawn on an Australian bank, and also UK, NZ and US cheques in the currency of the country of issue. Credit card charges are at the exchange rate current at the time of payment.

Photocopy and complete coupon below

☐ **Book Holder** ☐ **Metric Measuring Set**
Please indicate number(s) required.

Mr/Mrs/Ms _____

Address _____

_____

Postcode _____ Country _____

Ph: Business hours ( ) _____

I enclose my cheque/money order for $ _____ payable to ACP Publishing.

OR: please charge $ _____ to my ☐ Bankcard ☐ Mastercard

☐ Visa ☐ American Express ☐ Diners Club

Expiry date ____ /____

Card number

Cardholder's signature _____

Please allow up to 30 days delivery within Australia.
Allow up to 6 weeks for overseas deliveries.
Both offers expire 31/12/06. HLM4FI05

Food director Pamela Clark
Food editors Cathie Lonnie, Louise Patniotis
Nutritional information Amira Georgy
ACP BOOKS
Editorial director Susan Tomnay
Creative director Hieu Chi Nguyen
Senior editor Julie Collard
Designer Josii Do
Sales director Brian Cearnes
Publishing manager (rights & new projects) Jane Hazell
Brand manager Renée Crea
Sales & marketing coordinator Gabrielle Botto
Pre-press Harry Palmer
Production manager Carol Currie
Chief executive officer John Alexander
Group publisher Pat Ingram
Publisher Sue Wannan
Editor-in-chief Deborah Thomas
Produced by ACP Books, Sydney.
Printing by Dai Nippon Printing in Korea.
Published by ACP Publishing Pty Limited, 54 Park St, Sydney; GPO Box 4088, Sydney, NSW 2001. Ph: (02) 9282 8618 Fax: (02) 9267 9438. acpbooks@acp.com.au www.acpbooks.com.au
To order books phone 136 116.
Send recipe enquiries to Recipeenquiries@acp.com.au
Australia Distributed by Network Services, GPO Box 4088, Sydney, NSW 1028. Ph: (02) 9282 8777 Fax: (02) 9264 3278.
United Kingdom Distributed by Australian Consolidated Press (UK), Moulton Park Business Centre, Red House Road, Moulton Park, Northampton, NN3 6AQ. Ph: (01604) 497 531 Fax: (01604) 497 533 acpukltd@aol.com
Canada Distributed by Whitecap Books Ltd, 351 Lynn Ave, North Vancouver, BC, V7J 2C4, Ph: (604) 980 9852 Fax: (604) 980 8197 customerservice@whitecap.ca www.whitecap.ca
New Zealand Distributed by Netlink Distribution Company, ACP Media Centre, Cnr Fanshawe and Beaumont Streets, Westhaven, Auckland. PO Box 47906, Ponsonby, Auckland, NZ. Ph: (9) 366 9966 ask@ndcnz.co.nz
South Africa Distributed by PSD Promotions, 30 Diesel Road, Isando, Gauteng, Johannesburg; PO Box 1175, Isando, 1600, Gauteng, Johannesburg. Ph: (27 11) 392 6065/7 Fax: (27 11) 392 6079/80 orders@psdprom.co.za

Clark, Pamela.
The Australian Women's Weekly
4 Fast Ingredients

Includes index.
ISBN 1 86396 425 8

1. Quick and easy cookery.
I. Title. II. Title: 4 Fast Ingredients.
III.Title: Australian Women's Weekly.

641.5

© ACP Publishing Pty Limited 2005
ABN 18 053 273 546
This publication is copyright. No part of it may be reproduced or transmitted in any form without the written permission of the publishers.
Cover Prawn skewers with lime and green onions, page 20.
Stylist Yael Grinham
Photographer Rob Palmer
Home economist Liz Macri
Back cover at left, Fish fillets pan-fried with pancettta and caper herb butter, page 27; at right, Fettuccine with char-grilled vegetables, page 56.